Dance
Laugh
Eat
Cake

Jacqueline Landeen

Jacqueline Landeen

Also by Jacqueline Landeen

Headin' for the Sweet Heat,
Fruit and Firespice Cooking

First Edition

ISBN 0-966-3930-1-5

Library of Congress Card Catalog Number: 99-90555

10   9   8   7   6   5   4   3   2   1

Book Cover Design by Raymond Morales
Cover Author Photographs by John Slater
Edited by Caroll Shreeve

Distributed by Blessingway Books, Inc.
P.O. Box 31280
Santa Fe, New Mexico 87594
1-800-716-2953

www.blessingway.com

Published by
Bookin'
P.O. Box 1473
Park City, Utah 84060
1-800-573-6680, #88

www.bookn.com

Printed in the United States of America

For all the hungry hoofers

Dance
Laugh
Eat
Cake

. . . or is it lap dance, eat cake?

DANCE LAUGH EAT CAKE

DANCE   LAUGH   EAT   CAKE

RECIPES

Spring was never waiting for us, girl,
It ran one step ahead
as we followed in the dance
Between the parted pages we were pressed
in love's hot-fevered iron
like a striped pair of pants
MacArthur Park is melting in the dark
All the sweet green icing flowing down
Someone left the cake out in the rain
I don't think that I can take it
'cause it took so long to bake it
And I'll never have that recipe again
Oh No o o o o

"MacArthur Park" - A Tramp Shining
Words and Music by Jimmy Webb
(copyright © Dunhill Records, 1968)

INTRODUCTION

Softened by sleep, eating and moving are the two most persistent, active experiences in living. By merely opening and closing our mouths and moving our bodies, we maintain the continuation of life through food and our individual beat. . .*the* two constant reminders of our sexuality and sensuality. Tireless expressions in life triggered by emotions of love, hate, faith, hope, fear, sentimentality, aspiration, inspiration, greed, joy, sadness. The gamut from the gut. Like green ripening olives, eating and moving are always ready to give; incessant little benedictions that make every move a picture.

For too long, schizophrenic eating habits have been braided into our speed-addicted existence. As we cook less and obsess more about food, we further complicate things by losing—and now struggling to regain—the natural beat of life. Externally, the image of day to day living is all wrapped up like a tidy, complete package—no dirty fingernails allowed. No matter how perfect this image persists in portraying itself, it is actually an unnerving howl for help. Somebody stop me. With a two-by-four nerf bat, we are comfortably, steadily pounded upon by the seductive suggestion that we succumb to the speedy swoosh commanding us to just do it—just keep doing it. Just keep doing what? Aggress. Regress. It is no

small wonder that for many, the current concept of time is in warp speed swoosh terms rather than Brian Eno's Long Now appproach. The cake is taking too long to bake and yes, the chances are very good that we can't take it.

Faux eatmood: here, taste this. Dazed, empty taste buds. Faux eatmove: hey, tickle me. Stoic stiffness. What and how we eat along with when and how we move convey who we are as a culture. Living in a culture of anxiety and denial, we go from one lifeless swill to the next, rewarded in the work force with coveted security, which in reality, is false insurance. Dicing and crisping onions fills the loins with hope—this is real insurance.

The fear of food. A rankled rhythm. Confused and uncertain as to how we in America fell victim to the culinary culprit spreading cardboard cuisine evangelism from the ersatz food pulpit, we are good little soldiers, looking neither left nor right. Uninterested in the importance of a carefully, lovingly prepared meal. Uninterested in the importance of fellow human contact through snappy, vital rhythms.

But were we not head, heart, and spirit smart? Have we forgotten that head, heart, hand, and spirit are the impulse linkage to each other?

Take off the harness. Turn on the stereo. Point and click the remote to Peter Gabriel's *Steam.* Listen to the thumping infusion of energy filling your cooking space. Feel the musical steam against the kitchen steam. Smell it.

Taste it. Move. Catch a groove. Slice. Dice. Cook. Taste again. Do a few *real* eatmoves. Telephone the Dirty Dozen—friends and neighbors—for a dose of danceats. Insist they head on over to your impromptu Steam Café. Tell the Dozen they need to disentangle themselves from their tension and excess by taking a steam bath using the deep clean technique. Eating, laughing, dancing, sweating, restoring body bliss by natural oxygenation. Drag the sofa into the kitchen for a convenient, comfortable chase and collapse zone. When the Dirty Dozen arrives, dishfunction dance and get busy on creating the Dirty Dozen Dish. Get into that kitchen and rattle those pots and pans.

How about a simple spontaneous *tortilla filled with steamed sweet red peppers, coarsely chopped pears, Chimayo Caribe chile, ginger chips, and scads of pea sprouts with lots of roasted sesame seeds? Grab a beer that's been icing down in the bathtub. Or maybe a skinny baguette sandwich filled with smoked turkey, double cranberry chutney, walnuts and grated cheese wrapped in parchment paper and ready to travel . . . along with cold tumblers of limed Sportea.* Dance the oh so simple and sexy cumbio refining those tight, give-and-take pelvic moves that negotiate rhythms between partners. Trick hips, click, click, clicking to the saxy beat of Gato Barbieri's *Que Pasa.* Be liquid like a waterfall and via combusta all at once. Here comes the steady, slow sweet sweat. Now we are in zip-drive. Better than overdrive. *Where are the limes?*

Where is the lime cake? Avocado chantilly? Blackberry coulis? Danceats. Are we in the park yet? Are we shaking the tree yet? Swoosh time is now where it should be; in the Long Now. Dance. Culinary choreography has begun its course in the best possible place, your home, the Steam Café and Make Believe Grill. Just peel and invent—then reinvent the original intent. Laugh. Mix it all up with the yin and the yout . . . la vie continue. The recipe is back. Come in out of the rain. Eat cake.

GREAT THEATRE...
LOUSY FOOD

Pull up a chair. Let's talk. Trends are oppressive. Let's focus a gimlet eye on faddist food then stage a foodist protest. How about it? Restaurants have evolved from intimate, neighborhood hangouts to theatrical spectacles. Dark yet inviting back-door entry joints the likes of Pete's Pizza, where everyone caught up on each other's daily soap operas, while eating thin, hot and crusty pizza, thick with bubble-gum-like cheese, are on the wane. Food taste and food flavor have taken the back seat to formulaic décor and tired lighting in modern motif restaurants making for boring bourgeois dumps. Slick, unsavory restaurateurs mimic each other in an ongoing effort to hook the insatiable restaurant-loving public's pockets by exploiting their morphing, dining minds. Studied style with no food endurance.

Food that actually *enlivens* the tongue is under covert attack by the cardboard culprits. With carefully staged productions of entertainment and turn-key ambience, unidentifiable, inedible elements are served on platters, as the bells, whistles, and proverbial tap dance act begins. Green money is there because we think it is. Bad food is there because of the desire for money. Convenient, consensual reality. They got a routine, alla Burger King. Blatant Vaudevillian

hooks steer patrons away from the importance of what they are about to eat and toward theatrics of more holler-for-the-dollar results. Clever culinary capitalism. Catchy at first, this bloated Broadwayesque approach appeals to instant and temporary gratification, having spawned a stream swimming with self-proclaimed critics who in fact, critique non-stop and are sated by the hypnotic notion that it *is* darling to be critical.

Put down the banana. Forget saving the whales for now. Save your appetite which in turn might save our social spirit and each other. Love your bubble-gum-like cheese pizza. Hug the overworked, but still bouncy cook.

Good food is a result of simple, honest cooking minus the stage pomp and props. Great theatre does not make for or replace good food. Give me a bowl of linguine floating in extra virgin olive oil, cherry tomatoes, roasted garlic, and anchovy olives, obliterated with asiago cheese in a smoky, over-crowded café under naked light bulbs, not under the faraway elite Tuscan sun. Whether it's my place, your place, or the hard-to-find neighborhood café, it's winning womb food. Simple, succulent, satisfying and yeah, spiritual.

If food were to be used as the barometer of who and what we appear to be in America at the dawn of the year 2000, there are no clear signs that the spiritual fires are being stoked. Just a lot of lip service. How the hell have we been restoring ourselves, I ask. What kind of matter have we been putting into our mouths? Dismissing more curative choices of daily living, subliminal

advertising leads us to a non-existent utopia of what we should eat and what we should be. The coopoly of ad agencies fire their pounding salvos. And in the end, they have successfully created and marketed a truncated attention span of some 270 million Americans. Surface messages always welcome. Deep messages not allowed. Penetration is a punishable offense.

Staving off facing ourselves or failing to at least try and legitimately feed our spirits has been supplanted with blurred convenience. We no longer make time to rally around our ideas. Restaurants, keenly aware of this, religiously provide their version of a quick fix with entertainment and gratification to the impatient but abiding customer. This is not quick. This is quicksand.

Restaurants have become perfect pulpits in creating and convincing the eater of a new and challenged palate when in fact, it is a passive, non-surgical lobotomized palate. Not to speak of that elitist culprit, the jaded tongue. Those few restaurateurs who insist on quietly carrying the cooking torch crusading for delicious food first, money second or third in pecking order, do so unswervingly. Serving up that almost over used buzzword of a dish, *a passionata*, small is, more and more, scarce and special. The great theatre playwright Luigi Pirandello had it right. The imaginary fourth wall on stage respectfully separates the actor from the audience creating a protective scrim for each and all while being enriched.

In some ways, teensy intent cafés have a similar respectful 'wall'. A womb-like room within which the patron can eat and enjoy as the actors (waiters) serve and enrich the eaters with humble, tasty food offerings and beverages for the body in Café Citadel. A place to relax, and restore. Down with Ristorante Bogus with its wallpaper music and wallpaper food! Long live the hidden, relished riches of Café O.K. and the thrill of its simple, small, square grill. I know you've been there. This I know. There. I've gnawed enough on this bone. It's your turn.

Whisk and Wait Linguine
Serves Two

Handful of teeny cherry tomatoes

8 anchovy-stuffed olives

1 Tablespoon of roasted garlic cloves

2 oz. extra virgin olive oil

Juice of 3 oranges & juice of 1 lime

Whisk and wait

Until $\frac{1}{2}$ lb. of linquine is cooked al dente.

Drain linguine well

Stir Whisk and Wait concoction thru linguine

Obliterate with grated asiago cheese

Languish with Linguine and Your Lover.

HOT FEET...
COOL JAZZ

Are you with me? Go find your dancing shoes while we step this story out. Dance . . . groovy, snappy moves . . . toe-tapping, foot-stomping, hip-hopping, torso-gyrating, pelvis-pushing, head-bopping dance goes in and out of having a bad rap. Try as His Danceness John Travolta knee-slid down the stage in the film, *Saturday Night Fever*, with his spectacular, linear, seductive moves done in silky mohair, not all closet movers and shakers were seduced. *Saturday Night Fever* managed not only to create off-screen dance fervor and torpor but also dance disdain. City and country resistors alike were quick with slick, snide ridicule. Suddenly, dance was equated with disco, and disco was da worse! In several and sundry areas of America, would-be dancers were alienated from the dance floor. Dance seemed dormant. Here and there, spontaneous dancing, for many, acquired the subtle stigma that it was (is) uncool to move, really move to the beat, 'cause then you'd show your heat. So if you *did* move, you would reveal to all some deep, silly emotion, any emotion. Aloofness, detachment, iciness was the cool path to non-dance perfection. Hey man, dance then, now, and forever, *is* about stayin' alive.

Are we on the same frequency yet? If not, let's change channels and dial in together. Backstroke time with me. It's Friday night dance fever at the Holiday Ballroom (a misnomer for this jumpin' dance joint) in Windy City, Chicago, Illinois. The town that won't let you down. Next, Saturday morning live at Chicago Bandstand, jitterbugging and winking away to the viewers through the television camera lens, young primo dancers are inspired and duplicate gestures from the national watermark of dance shows, American Bandstand. Then, Saturday afternoon, live, at Record Hop, arm in arm with Irish boxer Michael, jukin' and jivin' to studio rhythms. It was a pattern every weekend in Chicago for dancing fools like myself, smile and sway Evonne, voice and hips Gerry, limber limbs Ronnie, The Fisherman Larry, and tall, handsome Chick, the rhythmic Guy Gumby. Devoted dance street rats from the 1960's. Forget yesterday's bop (first non-contact dance) and today's trend of non-contact line dancing. We deuce danced hand in hand, body with body, swapping, sliding, slithering, physical, emotional, and spiritual feelings with our partners until closing time. Contact. Chicago style. Whether slow or fast dancing, the gaze was always eye-to-eye while holding our excited breath. Alla tango eyes and sighs. Oh yeah. Now, think a minute. Can you recall a few, or maybe just one crystal-clear, good or bad, dance-floor memory? Warm feet. Warm heart. Leading with the loins. Unbelievable dedication to movement, the classic Chicago way. Looking back as well as

21

forward, the city of the hawk continues to possess a skulking, smooth testosterone pulse that is unrivaled, catching its windy thermals and never, ever, struggling with The Beat. It's no wonder that Michael Jordan tethered himself to this jock and jocular town in addition to being offered a contract in Chitown. Neighborhood dance energy still makes you want to groove and move, move and groove. Jazz oxford dancing shoes were ready to do their Friday night gig alongside cool jazz sounds at El Turk's (alias Big Daddy's), the Stork or the Sutherland Lounge. Two-inch Cuban heels made their merengue way to the El Mirador and Tito Rodriguez's primitive, bunched-up salsa sounds. Hot stepping street feet with googobs of dance routines lacing endless laughter and smooth, sexy moves. Sexy like Studs Terkel's words, while fluid and percussive. Sexy like Nelson Ahlgren's quiet photographs shouting saucy and strident Simone de Beauvoir. Defiant like Lenny Bruce at the Gate of Horn. Sweet and crunchin' like Gale Sayers, Walter Payton, Dick Butkus or an Italian cannoli. Like the country of Italy, the Chicagoan love affair with velocity. Movement everywhere. A midwestern Milano. Dance prospers in this pocket of pearls. Second City to none. Intense weekend dancing was pure, unadulterated feel-good butterfly release. Dancing provided the exhilarating detachment from problems and all of life's bad luck. Perfect. What better way to tackle the shackles of daily living? Not too seriously. Like Sinatra The Voice sang . . . it's the last dance . . . lsd . . . long, slow dance.

Make it last. Make no mistake. Living life by dancing through it and with it, along with all the other believing dancers out there, is campy comfort. And when tired of everything but the music, I want my dance card filled. Dance is the perfect lover. Dance is a life. Enduring its circling rhythms while on and off the floor, dance keeps the feet beating and free, the body ventilated and lubricated, the mind breezy, the psyche sexually plugged in. Don't short circuit. Keep your dancing shoes on. Wear them down. Wear them out. Dig the back beat. Hang with the hustle. Hot and cool. 2 cool. Stay alive. That's enough.

Deuce Dance Sandwich

Sauté 2 cups sliced Shiitake mushrooms

with 2 cloves minced garlic in

3 Tablespoons extra virgin olive oil until crisp

Souse with malt vinegar

Remove from heat

Press onto white or wheat bread

Eat with Black Currant Guinness Stout

Dublin Danceats for Two. Kickin.'

SCREENPLAY CAFÉ . . .
MAKE BELIEVE

Sweet 'n' Saxy Dance Café

Written and Directed by Jacqueline Landeen
All rights reserved. Copyright © 1996.

Multi-media performance play incorporating
food, dance, music, movement, song, stunts, style,
as odd characters mingle in a local jazz café.

Nine stage vignettes performed in 45 minutes.

Stage Vignette Sequence

Audience Entry Music   *Jazz at the Movies*

Actors Onstage   *Serenade to Sweden*
Entry Music

Vignette 1   Jazz People
Music   *Loud Minority*

Vignette 2   Early A.M. at Café
Actor Dialogue

Vignette 3   Auggie's Audition
Music   *Volupia*

Vignette 4   Angel Pipes Tells All
Actor Dialogue

Vignette 5   Kitsch Dream
Music   *Eagle Breaks*

Vignette 6   *Calling You*
Vocal Solo   Lisa Needham
Arrangement   Rich Wyman

Vignette 7   Cumbio Moods
Music   *Betty et Zorg*

Vignette 8   Beat Slam
Actor Dialogue
Music   *Egyptian*

Vignette 9
Actors Dance/Stunts
Music   *Pick up the Pieces*

Audience Exit Music   *Café Europa*

SOUND SCHEDULE

Aroma/sound effects during vignette (V) blackouts

Between V-1 & V-2	Italian roast coffee brewing.
Between V-2 & V-3	Café waiter whistling.
Between V-3 & V-4	Rapid, pounding, urgent-sounding door knocks.
Between V-4 & V-5	Low, slow fog changing to total, thick dream fog.
Between V-5 & V-6	Fog, coffee aromas.
Between V-6 & V-7	Café waiter mumbling, loudly griping, then whistling.
Between V-7 & V-8	Conga sounds, profuse incense aroma (sticks) waved and held by actors.
Between V-8 & V-9	Espresso machine making loud steaming sounds.

SWEET 'N' SAXY DANCE CAFÉ SOUND TRACK

Serenade to Sweden – Lew Tabackin

Loud Minority – United Future Organization

Volupia – Emerald Forest

End Titles – Eagle Breaks – Emerald Forest

Calling You
Sung by Lisa Needham
Arranged by Rich Wyman

Betty et Zorg – Betty Blue

Egyptian – Orchestra alla Siciliana

Pick Up The Pieces – Candy Dulfer

Café Europa – Deep Forest

VIGNETTE 2 – EARLY A.M. IN THE CAFÉ

Set-up Scene

Morning: Vic, owner of Sweet 'n' Saxy Dance Café, along with Scotch, the always mumbling, unhappy whistling Chicano waiter, and café patron/musician Auggie (a Long Island, N.Y. Italian character), are lumbering into the not-yet-opened-for business café, the neighborhood hangout.

Vic: Walks in, checks out café tables, chairs, floors, while enroute to center upstage table to do his bookkeeping and count cash. Pats Auggie (already seated at table having his morning coffee) on shoulder on his way upstage.

Hey, Auggie, how ya doin? Looks like things got busy for us after I left last night.

Auggie: Nods affirmatively. Slowly sipping his espresso and smacking his lips, leafing through the newspaper in cranky, sleepy, morning mode.

Vic: Sits down and begins calculating his bookwork.

Auggie: Hey Vic, without food (dunking biscotti into espresso), yeah, (bites into espresso-soaked biscotti), YOUR food, where are all of us gonna be, huh? Yuh know what I mean Vic?

Vic: Yeah.Yeah. I know what ya mean but all you artsy fartsy types come at me with all this philosophy shit. . .wait till you burn up from workin' as hard as I do, you won't care anymore. Instead of all those deep thoughts of yours, you'll be deep-frying french fries for a livin.

Auggie: Naw, naw Vic. I don't want to just put food in my body. I want to coo with pleasure as it makes its way into my mouth, man (takes another messy biscotti bite and moans).

Vic: Yeah, well keep moanin' and diggin' the pleasure, cause it's paying my monthly nut.

Scotch: Setting up tables, says in Chicano speak, Veek, what about my charge teeps. I got thees date tonight and I need some beeeans.

Vic: Ignores Scotch.

Auggie: So Vic, if these artsy fartsy types ain't so good for you – how come they pack the joint and you got the groovinest schmooze room in town?

Scotch: (Abruptly butts in) You wanna know why? I tell you why. . .cause I not just serveeng food here at Sweet 'n' Saxy, they all keep coming back for me (pompously points to himself), The Keed!

Vic: Scowl-stares contemptuously at Scotch and gets up to leave. Vic mutters, another wannabe macho artist full of himself and full of IT.

Auggie: (Shouts to Vic.) I got this conga-sax music ting I been working on . . . you got time to listen?

Vic: What kind of music? Like maybe something with female vocals?

Auggie: Why don't you just give a listen?

Vic: Whatever, fine . . . he starts to exit stage right . . . stops and glares back to Auggie, then deliberately points to Auggie and says . . . yeah, fine . . . but I want Angel Pipes (he exits). Fade to black.

VIGNETTE 4 - ANGEL PIPES TELLS ALL

Rapid, pounding succession of knocks on door are heard offstage right. Auggie keeps knocking, calling Angel Pipes' name in between knocks. Angel Pipes is half-singing, half-shouting, up and down the musical scale, rehearsing the song *Calling You*, holding and sucking a lemon in between notes. She does not hear Auggie knocking for several moments. Finally, he just opens door, barging into Angel Pipes' low-lit sparsely furnished loft with a simple, wide French chaise longue, placed down center right. Auggie then sees, and watches as Angel Pipes, in her pajamas, is singing her wild and free sounds along with flailing her arms. He physically stops her by grabbing her.

Auggie:	We got the gig.
Angel Pipes:	What gig? (continues to scat-sing)
Auggie:	Saturday night jam at Sweet 'n' Saxy.
Angel Pipes:	Yeah? . . .So.
Auggie:	Yeah. But there's a hitch.
Angel Pipes:	There's always a hitch . . . what's this one?
Auggie:	Without you, it ain't a go.
Angel Pipes:	I told you over and over Auggie. I'd never sing again at Sweet 'n' Saxy Dance Café.
Auggie:	Hey, what happened with you and Vic anyway, 'cause you're still wearing it Angel Pipes.

Angel Pipes:	I don't want to talk. I don't want to talk.
Auggie:	C'mon . . . what'ya got against Vic and Sweet 'n' Saxy, Angel Pipes?
Angel Pipes:	(Eye to eye intensity) I SAID I don't want to talk about any of it!
Auggie:	(Starts to walk over to chaise longue) Aw – don't get your panties all twisted.
Angel Pipes:	(This puts Angel Pipes over the top) Twisted?! Twisted?! (She now grabs Auggie by the arm) You wanna talk twisted? Vic is twisted . . . (now Angel Pipes is totally in Auggie's face. She then behaves as though she is in the confessional as her story rolls off her Catholic tongue.) Kneeling on chaise while making the sign of the cross to Auggie, then facing audience. Father forgive me, it has been four years since my last encounter with twisted Vic who thinks he's a chick (She turns to Auggie, tears in her eyes). You don't know how much I loved him.
Auggie:	Now sitting on chaise, and after pushing Angel Pipes to spill her story, he kicks into denial like a panty-waist and starts to get up. I don't know if I can listen to this.

45

Angel Pipes: Oh Yeah? You wanted to hear this Auggie (she shoves him back down onto the chaise.) So sit down, 'cause I'm gonna drive my train through your soft brain.

Black out #1 as Angel Pipes repositions herself on back side of Auggie. Lights come up. You want me to sing at this gig?

Blackout #2 as Angel Pipes moves to edge of downstage right. Lights come up. I'll sing if you get Vic to fess up and dress his chick thing once and for all. Ya see Auggie, knowing I still feel the way I do about him (expresses yearning love), I ain't so good at keeping his dirty little secrets. Angrily/sadly bites into her lemon. Black out.

Fruits and Nuts Dressed in Sweet Lemon
Serves Four

5 each, your choice 5 different dried fruits

$\frac{1}{2}$ cup sultanas (golden raisins)

Cover fruits/sultanas in water until plump

Drain water and place fruits in large pan

Cover with equal amounts orange/lemon juice

and sugar to taste

Simmer 30 minutes, add $\frac{1}{2}$ cup any nuts

and 1 tspn grated lemon rind

Remove from heat, cool

Eat with espresso, biscotti, or

Spoon on cream cheesed toast

Conga Line Canapes.

STEP BITES

Hey hepcats. Put the bite on. Catch a beat. Make it bitter. Make it sweet. Read, speak, or sing. Flip, flop, or fling. To the left. To the right. Step it up. Keep it goin'. It's alright. Hit your mark. Improve your groove. Don't let up. Be ready. Be very ready. Line up your talk with your walk. Walk the talk. Do the dog. Stance. Then dance. Step one, step two, if you don't step, well then who? Break through. Break down. Break dance. Forward left. Brush right. Side together. Back right. Brush left. Side together. Boxed in? Switch gears. Begin. Press palms to the floor. Now get going even more. Raise the shoulders. Up, down, up and down. O.K. Here comes 4/4. Tilt the head. To the left. Then the right. Add the sit move. Sit. Stand. Sit and stand. Bend the knees. Rotate hips front and right. The 1-2-3-4 corner delight. Then left. Rotate hips right in one count. Then left with a pelvis punch. Twist and turn. Turn up the thermals. Run for cover. Take it to the street. Hip and hop. Doo-wop, doo-wop. Throttle back. Throttle forth. Scrunch. Press. Move too fast, it won't last. Take it slow. It wants to grow. Nice and easy. Now let go. Ready to shift? Let 'er drift. Integrate. Attach a vocal gesture. OoAa. OoAa. Emancipate. Fire up the funk in between bites. Do the funky chicken. Wrap and roll. Breaker, breaker. Come in cumbio.

This is your mobile dance unit. We're in communication with your mobile food unit. *Feel* like fettucine. Too blind to see it? Too blind to see what you're doing? You're doing all the right things. You're on fire and people want to watch you burn. On the front burner. Feel the glow. Stay warm and chile. It'll flow. Focus on the footsteps and fromage. Be a kitchen dummy with happy feet, happy tummy. That's everything there is short of honkin' hoof beats.

Start dancing. Stop eating. Start eating. Stop dancing. Start stepping. Stop biting. Start biting. Stop stepping. Mix it all up. Thump. Pound. Chew. Crunch. No pasta. No pulse. The beauty of an appetite. ini food. itti food. Here come the vibes. LSB. The long slow bite. LSS. The long slow step. Distinction cake. Lick sorbet. Crumb bums. Dim sum. Onion. Gumbo ya ya. Dance the frittata. Without marijuana. Veggie this. Veggie that. We gratefully accept your cash. Garlic grits. Homemade chips. Step-by-step. Bit by bit. Swing, squeeze, twist, salsa. Pass the juicy, stuffed poblano. Hot. Black. Sweet. Strong. Cajun coffee goin' down. Move. Grind. Jitter. Jump. Honey-drippin' fritter. Rant has its own rhythm. Rhythm its own rant. Here is the message. Here is the slant. Down and out? Don't need no clout. Cook humble. Cook quick. Cook out. Serve a dish of dissonance. Find out what it's all about. Bite-size. Boulder-size. Get the news to your tribe. Bang out some steps, make 'em glide. Point your hips, clap your hands, click your heels, kick and slide. Follow an example. Flamenco food.

Gypsy pride. Take your time. Step and bite. Go with the tide. Dance, scamp. Do the scampdance. You know what I'm talkin' about. Get jiggy wid it. Have you hit your groove? You got it. Now eat and move.

Funky Chicken Hash
Serves Two

Process 1 boned chicken breast to smooth

Mix into chicken, 2 minced garlic cloves

1 Tablespoon grated lemon rind

2 Tablespoons fresh/chopped basil

Sauté chic mix on high heat until crisp

Spoon chic on green leaf lettuce leaves

Wrap and Roll.

Get communal.

Pass the hash around.

Do the Mash.

Thai Tea Time.

GRAFFITI GRUB

graffiti, n., pl.: inscriptions/drawings on a public surface

grub, v.: to clear or root out by digging; n. slang for food.

Wall scrawls, scratches, and scribbles that evoke raw and free dance patterns or oscilliscope-like brain strolls. Born from the people, highly innocent and intelligent youth wanted to say something. Graffiti culture was what these visual mutes had to offer to express themselves. Graphic graffiti voices have persisted to exist through the years in spite of society's insistence to silence on-the-surface seemingly schizoid swirls. A visual vernacular, the movement of graffiti fed on its own unique raw, root food. Nightshade food. Janked (messed-up), spray-painted messages were responded to with disdain, disgust, and reciprocal spray-painted disappearance. Over and over again, the moving, moony patterns waxed and waned. Slamming down a spiked coffee, beer, or straight whiskey shot, then a cheese-chili dog chased with French fries, graffiti guerrillas cruised a midnight run under the night sky canopy while the world was dead asleep. Digging deep into their graffiti crusade, they displayed singularly individual activism. Like dogs territorially spotting, they left their

marks. Higher-ground hieroglyphics were visible wherever there was a wall, door, or surface that screamed, 'graffiti me'. Bad ballet with good, mean rhythm. Creative pimples waiting to be popped. Like it or not, graffiti was quick to elicit instant response. The mission of graffiti, to shock, slam, alarm, and repel, was not only successful but bred its own beat, thriving on mutual reverse hostility. Janky, juicy juxtaposition. A rebellion with a covert rhythm. The graffiti bridge had been built and was ready for traffic.

Graffiti made its way down the birth canal, was born, proliferated and prospered. Like a beautiful Bruce Marden or Arthur Adelmann abstract painting, the young graffitists used spray cans instead of artist brushes or sticks to paint their beautiful, rough image-messages, messages that forced the brain to think, and think hard. Graffiti guerillas became invisible graffiti gurus proselytizing wicked, wild, and scenic visual images. Initially considered disrespectful wall defacing in America, these in-your-face gnarly, cave-like graphic hooks, tails and symbols, yanked the onlooker's attention. Graffiti began to evolve as its own definitive art medium showing up in eventual mainstream works of artists such as Keith Haring. Graffiti visions steamed steadily along showing up in public and private spaces shouting its grass roots commentary. Some were common graffiti with nothing to blow your skirt about. Others were exquisite and made you want to capture the image through photography. Early graffiti's lack of any seeming clarity was a clarion

call of what was to come down along the road; graffiti, gothic, gargoyle. While the masses of Stepford-like androids slept-walked through life, numbing themselves to real movement, blissful in their self-imposed state of inertia, graffiti was the wake-up call that failed to awaken but has ultimately succeeded in resuscitating these hearts without a beat. A small g-feat. Root food was unearthed and on the cultural move. No potatoes. No pulse. Jumpy, erratic, polyrhythmic and polytonal graffiti resembling John Cagey-like movement scratched its poignant, powerful muted path into the dead air mainstream of the true mutes.

A suggestion for those who continue to resist. Take a hint from Mexico's celebration of the Day of the Dead. You can eliminate vandalism and graveyard graffiti. Move into the cemetery. Bring nightshade food. Potatoes, peppers, tomatoes, garlic, and chiles will be what speaks to you. Grub first, then ethics. Have respect. Don't feel like going forward? Don't feel like going back? Can't find your ego with two hands? Learn to be a visual mute. Feel the Braille beat. Feel your pulse. Then listen to your heart beat. Mark your spot. You're safe here at Cemetery Café. For awhile.

Gazpacho Nightshade Salad
Serves Four

Bake 2 red potatoes

Peel, seed, chop 1 cucumber

Chop 2 tomatoes and $\frac{1}{2}$ onion

Chop 1 small red and green sweet pepper

Mince 3 cloves garlic fine

Place all ingredients in bowl

Add 3 Tbspns extra virgin olive oil

Juice of two oranges and 1 lemon

Toss and coat

Fork-mash potatoes into 4 portions

Spoon salad/gazpacho juices onto potato mash

Eat with serrano chiles and breadsticks

Graffitist Grub for the Graveyard.

WORKING MAN'S BAR

Attenzione! Mangiare! Stand-up and eat. Like storming birds, working men and women from all walks of Italian life arrive daily in enthusiastic, expressive swarms for breakfast, lunch, and mid-day appetizers at small, inexpensive, local 'bars'. Dotted through the cities and countryside of Italy, they are reminiscent of an American neighborhood endangered species, the tavern, except well-lit. Animated, chicly-dressed Italiani casually eat and drink while leisurely socializing and standing in these welcoming bars. Bringing each other current on local politics and gossip, they enjoy each morsel washed down with their beloved miracle water and chased with espresso, cappuccino, ristretto, or corretto. They wear that charming, civilized pace of grace and ease even though life appears *troppo in fretta* (too fast). Sated and stimulated all while standing and eating in their home away from home, they're now ready to return to work in a slow, strolling style—*bella figura*—as though they have let go and are holding on to letting go. *Andiamo! Calma!* Tricky little eatmove. The ever-stylin' stroll. Sign me on for beginner through advanced classes. Hopefully, 500 years of Italian ancestry will not be required.

Sit down and eat. Then deal the cards. American workers, on the other hand, can be seen taking their meals half-sitting down in neighborhood or downtown joints where customers quaff quickly, merely out of necessity, while half-socializing. Better some social connection than none. The working man's bar is whatever establishment may be closest to the job. Perhaps a local, womby tavern sporting an aged, leftover sign reading Smoking Allowed Here with an outdoor ditch lily alley garden. On the long, polyurethane bar that could double for a wet siesta slab, pickled eggs and pickled pig's feet glow like aliens in gallon jars. Mesmerized, bar patrons trip on the phosphorescent, undulating, lava lite glow. Surreal, alien food. Amusement food. Like eating the requisite hot dogs and soft pretzels at a baseball, football, basketball, or hockey game. Jiffy food mopped up with beer. Quick and dirty. Fast, tasty, unspecific food. A place where one doesn't have to get too specific anyway because the neighborhood psyche believes the deeper you dig, the unhappier you'll be. An organic hangout allowing plenty of time and space to sub-surface or resurface one more time and be missed as well as welcomed back. A place to blink back the tears or howl and flail in joy or, when the joint gets jumpin', pick a fight. Yeah. No real harm intended. Just a healthy joust. A place where everyone vibrates like a tuning fork and eats their Stout Cake without forks. Alive, anti-social, meaningful behavior. Unforgettable American neighborhood macholism.

Attracted to each other, strong men and women with excellent peripheral vision, are walking/eating violations. Always busy scrubbing their souls. Deliciously clumsy, but still good form. America's version of Italy's *bella figura*. Lots of density. Male and female cronies building strong bones and bodies here at the Beckoning Bar in the U.S.A. Where unstudied hip and intense go together. Uncompromised. Unconstipated. No wet diapers allowed. Drink the stout. Eat the stout cake. Dispel the fatigue of thinking. Something's about to shake loose. Chow for now. Then park and hold your spot at the table or bar. Restored and ready. Glowing like those pickled eggs on the bar. Working men. Working women. Working bars. Weathering each other. Work makes life sweet. Good gluten. Not a part of a maladjusted mainstream. Not another fern bar. No mineral water. Honey-tongued and stouthearted. It takes time to catch up with visionaries.

Stout Cake for the Lover Stout Hearts

2 cups flour

1 cup softened butter

1 cup brown sugar

1 tspn baking powder

1 tspn cinnamon

1 tspn nutmeg

3 eggs – $\frac{1}{2}$ pint stout beer

1 Tbspn grated orange rind

1 cup currants

Pulse-blend softened butter into flour until grainy

Add dry ingredients

Whisk eggs with beer

Blend egg/beer mixture into dry ingredients

until smooth

Stir in orange rind and currants

Pour into buttered, floured 9-inch pan

Bake at 350 degrees for 40 minutes

Demands to be dunked

Keeps its punch

Working Bar-worthy Sweet Tack.

KITCHEN RHYTHM...
KITCHEN CHAOS

Ms. Hip. She can dance. She's got rhythm. She can cook. But she cain't walk. Sometimes slipping, sliding, tripping, or falling, the word klutz fits in there somewhere. For some and sundry dancers, this trait leftover from rigorous years of first through fifth ballet position, i. e. forced foot turnout, sometimes results in a defensive catchy move called the proud duck waddle walk. As the feet step wide, open, and out, the legs, like pistons, display strong, sexy and knobby calves and the glutes bump up and down and up and down. I kinda have dug wearing this disciplinary dance-stamp of paid dues. Ay yai yai. Forget about it. Now in my kitchen, well, anything goes. No matter if you cain't walk. There are no secrets here. Talk about total freedom and safety. I can dance the duck moss waddle or whip that berry cream fool in the kitchen and be the fool. Moving and dancing the kitchen talk while in Kitchen Central can be heady improvisation as well as body participation. When Jack Nicholson and Jessica Lange gave the eloquent love-making performance (mess is best) in the all-time kitchen scene of the classic film, *The Postman Always Rings Twice*, kitchens were anointed with new, wicked respect. Long live flour-dusted thick, deep, butcher block tables. Sturdy kitchen colonels.

Indispensable, individual solid beds of wood when it comes to chopping, cooking, eating, dancing, and making love. Long a nuclear-free zone, kitchens are those benevolent, forgiving spaces that maintain their untouchable identity, daring whomever to be well-oiled and on notice for real life. I'll take my sorrows straight and in the kitchen. Places where personalities are formed and then, oddly and openly function. Talk, complain, vent, gripe, shout, cry, laugh, giggle, disgust, touch, punch, duke it out, then eat. Flying food tools. Landing food drool. KitchensRule.com. What about yours? Pay attention, you'll pick up on finding your own rhythm and chaos. Stick with it. Check it out. Nothing to cook? Be resourceful. Fake it like the less fortunate yet thankful.

Empty the cupboards. This is, after all, Kitchen Central. There has to be something hanging around for just this food moment. Use that funky fruit to make pineapple pancakes or waffles. Make stew over surprise. Then sit and stew at the kitchen table with friends, family, lovers. Watch as the devil, cad, angel, madonna, and food fight in us all wildly erupts in peels and squeals without missing an impromptu, chaotic beat. Wraparound sound. There it is. Kinetic kitchen karma, KiKiKa, baby talk. Filling your mind with mischievous thoughts and actions. Why not? Humor is more and more on the wane. Kitchen humor is a lasting tonic. It gets us through the good, bad, and ugly. God forbid there should be any unchecked moroseness in the

recesses of anyone's brain synapse upon entering Kitchen Central. Because it will be leeched out like unwhisked egg whites, all runny, viscous, and plopping where it will. Face it. Kitchens are kitsch. Clean or cluttered. Or with just one lonesome stove. The all-purpose hearth to cook on, keep warm by, hang clothes on to dry, tell stories around, eat, drink, and dance around. No spiritual famine or malaise going on here. Kitchens give good *gemütlichkeit*.

Now, about emptying those cupboards. Better yet, strip the kitchen of its excesses. Pare way down. Then Ms. Hip, strip yourself. Joe Cocker-style. Baby take off your dress. Yes. Yes. Layer by layer. You can't sing the blues unless you been blue. Like a delicious raspberry, banana, whipped-cream-tiered cake being eaten. Piece by piece.

What about you Sir Hip? Baby, take off your shirt. Flirt. Flirt. Make rhythm. Make chaos. Make mess. Make mousse. Well Ms. Hip and Sir Hip, let's have a merger. It's not what you acquire, it's what you give up. Stay the nudist foodist you now are. Suck on popsicles in the bathtub. Conga back to Kitchen Central. Refuel. Do the popsicle push. Linger in out-of-code. Swap emergency food interviews, soon to be on the learning channel. Turn your knobs on. You can leave your hat on.

Nudist Foodist Avocado Mousse for Four

Two small ripe avocados

$\frac{1}{2}$ cup superfine sugar - Juice of $\frac{1}{2}$ lemon

Two egg whites

1 cup heavy cream

Raspberry or any red jam

Peel and pit avocados

Blend avocados with sugar/lemon until smooth

Finger-lick for taste-tease

Whip cream/egg whites separately till stiff

Pile part of cream and whites onto avocado purée

Gently fold into each other until messed

Fold remaining cream/whites into avocado

Smear some red jam on plate

Plop avocreamo atop

Looks like love.

Tastes like bananas.

Avocado's Avocation . . . Slip/Slide Food

COFFEE CULTURE 2000

Question directed to person on the street:
What does Coffee Culture 2000 mean for you?

Point. Click. Cappuccino. Gobs of cyber cafés loaded with laptops and lattes. Camel Cigarettes. Techno-music. A *Blade Runner* life jacket. Friends don't let friends drink coffee at Starbucks. The return of simple social connections~coffee, poetry, games, conversation.

The Internet, and with my coffee closeby, who needs to travel? Coffee chic taken to the extreme sterile scene. Futuristic tribes of extreme caffeinds. Pretension. Hypertension. Caffeine-like tension. Coffee and cyber culture devouring itself. Flavored IV's. Coffee health insurance. Coffee and food will not unite the world.

Coffee congregations. Coffee node bars with Bill Gates' replicants. Tall, dark, voluptuous, foamy. Small, skinny, sensuous, marshmallowy. Part coffee. Part cyber. Part Chinese. Pacific Rimmy. Liqueur-laced coffees. Cappuccino, espresso, latte pills. Chewable, artificially-flavored coffee vitamins. Computed coffee. Syringe-injected coffee. Cyberized coffee. Implanted coffee chips. NASA-style dehydrated floaty coffee packets. Espresso in travel bottles . . . like booze. Rolling American Spirit cigarettes. Coffee amusement parks with huge coffee cup rides.

Politically correct coffee galleries with bad coffee propoganda. Controlled coffee laws. Coffee detox houses. Coffee steam bath houses. Mocha-tized. Violations. From Fahrenheit 451 to Coffee VIOL8. Coffee criminals. Coffee: a receding horizon. Coffee guerillas. Like a coffee moth, the flame I fly toward. No shoes, no shirt, no service, no dancing, no breathing . . . coffee served by appointment only.

What to sweat. What to let go. But not espresso. Nature knows how to compute better than the digital restrictive model. Now and in 2000. One Americano coffee please. Harnessing wattage of shoe energy (walking) after coffee. Measuring body data after drinking espresso. Attaching digital gestures to physical gestures after drinking coffee. Hard-bitten, heat-seeking coffee police. Throttle back emphasis on money. Throttle up coffee. Coffee zipcode to coffee zip-code. Coffee culture 2000? It's not that tidy.

Survival. Breast-stroking in the sand or water-skiing in the dirt. Coffee will help. Coffee-love connection. Artificial coffee cowboys and cow-girls. Organic, schmorganic coffee. Coffee karma. Cosmic coffee. Coffee made with swamp water. More greed, more profit. Coffee speaks to me now, it will in 2000. Bitter beans are better. Like the borscht circuit, a coffee circuit. Coffee dere-licts. Coffee talk-shows. Coffee antibiotics. Cof-fee-coated plastic binkies. Don't talk to me about coffee. It's an unnatural, unecessarily stimulating beverage. Coffee choristers. Coffee chatter. Brain chatter. Juicy coffee juju. Speedy,

zenny meditation with movement. Breakthrough decaf that replaces sleeping pills. Non-specific warm, brown water. Android coffee. Rationed, licensed, tagged coffee beans. Coffee served in silver paper pouches with straws. Instead of pool hustlers, coffee hustlers. Coffee clubs with white and coffee-colored singers. No brain refrain without the daily a.m. coffee drill.

A superior manic mocha. Coffee dances for professional coffee depressives. 21st century Capuchin Monk Cafés. Faxing cappuccino. Energy that seems to be going everywhere but in fact goes nowhere, just a lot of arrows. E-coffee. Let it reveal itself. The more things change the more they stay the same. Castaneda coffee awareness. Block anticipation. Carpe coffee. Hit escape.

Carpe Coffee Pôt de Crème
Serves Six

Preheat oven to 325 degrees

2 cups heavy cream

$\frac{1}{2}$ cup sugar

1 tspn vanilla

4 Tbspn strong (or espresso) coffee

6 egg yolks

Scald cream, don't let boil.

Stir sugar and coffee in cream until dissolved

Add vanilla

Beat egg yolks until pale in color

Slowly add to cream, stirring constantly

Strain into 6 baking cups/crocks

Place cups in baking pan half-filled with hot water

Bake 35 minutes

Chill. Chase with chocolate-laced black coffee.

Cut and paste to Y2K Coffee Culture Clipboard.

ROSARY OVER MINESTRONE

Let me thicken the broth. As best remembered, the story goes something like this. A little girl's head is bowed in supplication. Her hands are clamped, fingers proudly pointing to the heavens, chestnut-auburn hair floats like long, silk threads across her dark Turkish-like eyes. She steadfastly reveres her beautiful, silver-haired grandmother Francesca, whose rosary beads are laced through her slender fingers, about to invoke the red-blooded, hard-working carpenter and family man, St. Joseph. San Giuseppe, we pray for peace and grace and spiritual food, for wisdom and guidance—for all these are good. But don't forget the potatoes. Or the minestrone. Or the bread to strengthen our hearts. This simple table prayer summoned the saints quickly, reassuring the family that saints were always present to preserve and protect. Convinced of this unique brand of prayer power, I sensed St. Joe was at our table, his table now, breaking and passing bread, then sipping red wine with us. So soft, like colored air, his presence communicated kind authority. He steered and spurred our social, spiritual thought during the supper hour. Ever-supportive of the underdog and emancipation of the undervalued soup cooks, no-nonsense St. Joseph remains a loyal friend and partner to this day.

Growing up Catholic, one was continuously reminded that religion and food were/are one within each other, the Holy Unity living alongside the Holy Trinity. A modest generalization. Religion represented spiritual food and food was/is its own religion. Catholicism. Foodism. A Moebius menu participated in on a strict, daily basis. Mass was attended every morning by sleepy young women with mantilla-covered heads, rosaries ever handy. Communal and contemplative. Solid Benedictine ingredients. Eager to be in and out of the confessional booth of truth, long or short penance was performed depending on the previous week's sins. Extra points (minimal penance) was conferred for good Catholic girl behavior, the butt of constant jokes, the kind Frank Zappa sang and quipped about. You know, Catholic girls, with their tiny little mustache . . . about face. Consciences now cleared, we were ready to eat heavenly, airy, golden, honey-glazed donuts and drink milk from petite cartons. Simple sweets eaten with thanks and bowls of laughter. Now, add some old and mossy Italian heritage to this recipe and you have fired-up Cathletic Foodies. Playful religious respect was engaged for yet another delicious eggplant, ham & swiss baked sandwich goin' down at lunch time. All the while leaping, jumping and athletically trying to catch glimpses thru classroom door windows of inaccessible hunks and heels. Gorgeous Catholic guys marching through our side of the school to lunch in our cafeteria. Mouths watering along with mouthfuls of food,

the words, it's you and me Babe, rolled off our tongues in typical, sinking style as the males paraded by. Female foodie flirts we were. Indelible imprints that never failed to overwhelm us with the interwoven mysterious enjoyment of life, food, and the percolation of boy-girl-boy juices. Such bodily churning was frequently evidenced by blackish blue love badges on some of the necks of the good, tough girls known as the sexy DOBS, Daughters of the Blue Sweaters. Cocky Catholic chics. They knew how to live, love, laugh, dance, and eat in all their hormonal glory. I quietly yearned to be part of their singularly, sassy club. Unhinged, unharnessed, and proudly unholy as they sprinkled themselves daily with the obligatory holy water.

In later years, questions such as what's cooking and what's to eat would frequently be spoken somewhere between the tenth Hail Mary, first Our Father, Ave Maria or sticky Maria. Ready to hop on the flavors of food at the table, grace before meals could be anything from whose food? your food? my food! or your God, my God, oh God. Then pass the pasta, cheese, and fried olives please. During and after meals, the commotion of eating encouraged the fall from grace to grimace with comments like, who ate all the hot, creamy polenta? Followed with, I got three words for you, ther-a-py. Now pass what's left of the min-i-strohn, you cav-a-dil. You still seeing that chic, An-i-sette? That was it. Out came nonni's rosary slammed onto the table as the final saving grace at the end of the meal. The ongoing supper sport

of Sicilian sarcasm abruptly ended with her symbolic pile of rosary beads now peering at us like wet, black beans. They begged to be eaten or tossed in the minestrone when the half-joking, half-serious opportunity presented itself. Spontaneous, sacrilegious behavior was better than sanctimonius, pious posture.

Going with the gut. Balls up. Hard-core inspection was the key, still is. Human beings mouthing off to each other as a form of checks and balance. Everyday. At supper. Affectionate abuse. St. Joseph would give his nod of patient and humorous approval. So before eating minestrone or any other soup, and especially if the trusty rosary is not handy, bow your head and cross (bless) your soup. Make mine a double minestrone with a double blessing. For the heck of it, throw in a few black beans to stave off the penance blues. Give humble beans a chance. Enjoy the blessed soup in all its simmered goodness. Taste its dark and rich flavors. Break and drag big chunks of crusty bread through the strone soup. Crunch and chew on fresh, crisp, fennel root. Respect rosary food. Prepare for a biting banter at the supper table. Healthy cathletic conflict. Like making the sign of the cross before and after eating. Like an obedient monk or nun. It brings good luck no matter what your religious persuasion. Toast the rosary by clinking glasses of Gavi wine lemonade. Twist the rosary around your wrist like a Tibetan mala. Give universal thanks. Then just keep on giving. Like St. Joseph. *Alla hospitaliano.*

Zuppa di Minestrone
Serves Six

3 strips bacon/pancetta, 4 cloves garlic,

1 onion, diced

1 cup each carrots, potatoes, 2 tomatoes, chopped

3 cups each freshly squeezed orange juice & water

$\frac{1}{2}$ medium cabbage, chopped

1 cup peas, 1 cup cooked white (canellini) beans

1 cup cooked al dente acini di pepe or any teeny macaroni

4 Tbspn freshly torn basil

Asiago or Fontinella cheese

Sauté bacon, garlic, onion in soup pot, drain oil

Add carrots, potatoes, tomatoes to bacon mixture

Stir in orange juice/water

Simmer 40 minutes or until flavor is rich

Add cabbage, peas, beans and macaroni

Cook 15 minutes until done

Float lots of basil and freshly grated cheese

Mangiare min-i-strohn with a big wooden spoon

Rosary Riffs Are Optional.

DANCE   LAUGH   EAT CAKE

PICNIC FOR
STARVING ARTISTS

Art is a wicked thing—it is what we are. Art is everywhere, figuring out what's in front of it, what's in back of it. Like a colossal Robert Rauschenberg canvas; spewing, questioning, flitting, and forcing viewers to rethink what and how they think. Art opens us up, out and around. Like an aging, beautifully rusted, gnarled wire, lost and forgotten on a lonely beach, art exhibits years of water and wind-polished, free, flowing, abstract images ushering in subliminal thoughts to the curious onlooker through an off-guard art lens. If life copies art, it often chooses kitsch. And no matter how shoddy, i.e., kitschy, the art form appears . . . it is the intent to express that merits notice.

As with art, artists proclaim what they are about. In Medieval times, artists and craftsmen told the spiritual stories behind architecture and paintings. They were well thought of, if not revered. What have artists come to mean in modern society? Perhaps fancier garrets, tucked neatly away down an alley, upstairs over a garage. Not surprisingly, insulated and living alternatively. Kudos to those enduring, oh so admirable artists who live/work their art for art's sake. Busy creative bees gardening their lives from where they are inspired, deep down inside where the art

spirit lives, producing heady honey. Ascetic advocates who profess and practice conviction rather than convenience, that delightfully non-existent word in poetry or art.

For those on the planet who do not understand, accept, or recognize this awesome spirit in artists as well as a similar innocence in animals, human nature continues to rear its ugly head, attempting to cage both groups out of imaginary fear. In the animal instance, it might be done physically and in the artist instance, on an innocuous level. The predictable behavior pattern of non-acceptance and rejection becomes a safe knee-jerk societal response. Alas, nothing can forever suppress the voices of true arcane artists. No matter how underground artists may be, their message surfaces and resurfaces with ever greater power and mystery. They are resourceful and resilient. *Artistico in Purgatorio.* The thing is, they believe in their art form solidly enough to know, unequivocally, their time to shine will arrive. These tenacious artists will exit the fiery grave with shy, sailing glory, knowing full well that there can be only so much temporal control and then, the brilliant creative karma of suffering releases and ascends.

Starving artists are only a little bit hungry. They can run on half-full. It's about survival. We could all similarly stay a bit hungry and nervous through life. It would be good for us. Less being more would take on meaningful proportions. We have acquired the hapless habit of selective memory when it comes to suffering. We forget

about others. We lock or leave people out. We need a good dose of suffering. Artists are no strangers to this concept. They are soldiers of service and suffering. Mind you, they do not have a unique ticket to the Pity Bus. But I ask the question, how can we ever attain true spirituality if we don't feed and care for our fellow man on a basic everyday level? Money, love, or food does no good unless you spread it around. What's good making a dollar if you don't do anything with it? And although dollars may delude one into thinking he or she has more rights than others, with those rights come responsibility. Being suspect and cranky of oneself and one's worth is healing and humbling. It reminds us of our unifying mortality. Using the Alan Watts notion, artists are able to let go without becoming loose yogurt. They do not suffer from, hey, this far and no more! It's more like, don't talk to me about ephemeral, get me excited about eternity!

For artists, picnic food with exciting humility will do the trick. Herbal magic. Pure, parsimonius picnic power. Nettles. Salmonberries. Desert creosote tea. Peas and love. Getting back to tasty basics. Strolling through a fragrance garden, with our minds free of the prophylactic, psychic membrane. Like a boar sniff, sniff, sniffing for truffles, or getting drunk on the scent of orange blossoms or orange flower water. Flat-out flower power. Artists live each day with the reality that more and better illusions do not exist. There is no perfect healing in store for them yet they unknowingly are able to see and hear the genie in themselves.

DANCE   LAUGH   EAT CAKE

Artists stop, look, and do a better dance. They trust and can leave the bird cage door open. And rather than flying with buzzards, they choose to soar with eagles. Armed with a pocket picnic of chives, wild herbs, and berries to nourish them, they enact conviction versus convenience, avoiding complacency. A perfectly imperfect picnic.

Hence, the artist's pillow is seldom empty. From Bartok to pillow talk, their inner life libido is never finito. Unfamished, sated artists. They know to *be* as well as to *do*. They know that to live is to fly. Hands Up! Complete surrender. Catch, then release. Dance, laugh, eat. Like making love, you think of nothing else.

Foraged Nettle Frittatta for Four

Steam 2 cups nettles

Drain, wring out and chop coursely

Saute crisp $\frac{1}{2}$ cup chopped onion over campfire

Whisk 6 eggs

Add 3 Tbspn grated Asiago Cheese

Blend all ingredients

Coat iron skillet with 3 tbspn. olive oil

Pour nettle/egg mixture in skillet

Cook over campfire until fluffy or

bake at 350 degrees for 30-40 minutes

Tastes like a spinach and green tea omelet

Push your palate

Brew nasty survival desert creosote tea

Pick/eat pink, nectary, salmonberry flowers

Still Hungry? Stay Hungry.

You Won't Starve.

When I dance, I forget myself, I am danced.

Marge Piercy